THE BRITISH MUSEUM
CHINESE
LOVE POETRY

THE BRITISH MUSEUM
CHINESE
LOVE POETRY

EDITED BY

Jane Portal

THE BRITISH MUSEUM PRESS

For Claire

Translations reprinted by permission of the copyright holders where available
(see p. 96)

Calligraphy by Qu Lei Lei
Photography by British Museum Department of Photography and Imaging

First published in 2004 by The British Museum Press
A division of The British Museum Company Ltd
38 Russell Square, London WC1B 3QQ
www.britishmuseum.co.uk

Reprinted 2004, 2006, 2007

A catalogue record for this book is available from the British Library

ISBN-13:   978-0-7141-2413-1

Frontispiece: Seated beauty with a clock, 1873, Qing dynasty.
Woodblock print, ink and colours on paper.

Designed and typeset in Centaur by Peter Ward
Printed in China by C&C Offset Printing Co., Ltd

INTRODUCTION

THE THREE ARTS of poetry, calligraphy and painting are regarded in China as the Triple Excellence, a happy combination brought together in this small book. Each poem or extract is given in English translation and illustrated with an appropriate image selected from the collection of the British Museum and accompanied by a phrase of Chinese calligraphy by Qu Lei Lei. The subject of the poems is love, in all its variations: love for husbands and wives, family and friends, times and places as well as poems of courtship, parting and passion.

Poetic tradition

The poetic tradition in China is extremely rich and is interwoven into its history from earliest times in a continuous line to the present day, as shown by the inclusion here of poems by Chairman Mao, who was an accomplished poet and calligrapher. Poetry is usually associated with male scholar-officials, who were given a thorough education in the classics in order to pass the civil service examinations, but it was also written by emperors and court ladies, monks and soldiers, as well as by simple folk. The latter probably spoke or sang the earliest poems and, in fact, Chinese poetry has always been closely related to music. The earliest works in this selection come from *The Book of Songs* or *Book of Odes (shijing)*, compiled in about 600 BC, supposedly by Confucius, and possibly dating back several centuries earlier. These are folk songs and ballads, festive songs and hymns, and some would have been accompanied by music and dance. Love and courtship are recurrent themes, although the songs centre on daily activities such as farming, hunting and going to war. Remonstrance against social injustices also features. These simple love and courtship songs were sometimes interpreted as allegories by later Confucian scholars. Many are highly compressed and a number start with an image from nature, such as a bird or insect or plant, which parallels or contrasts with the human feelings expressed. The songs usually consist of lines of four characters or syllables arranged in verses of four, six or eight lines, with rhymes at the ends of the even-numbered lines. *The Book of Songs* or *Odes* became one of the Five Confucian Classics because of its great antiquity and its link with Confucius. Despite the complicated studies and commentaries on these songs by later scholars, the simple passions and concerns expressed have a timeless quality.

Another example of early poetry in China is the *sao* tradition of southern China, which may have derived from shamanistic chants and was compiled into the *Chu Ci* or *Songs of Chu* in the first century AD. Amorous encounters between male and female gods and shamans and exotic imagery provide a contrast with the northern *Book of Songs*. Long descriptive prose-poems called *fu* were a feature of the Han dynasty (206 BC–AD 220), as were anonymous folk songs called *yuefu* after the Music Bureau set up in about 120 BC. A new form of poem called *shi* emerged during the Han dynasty and became dominant in the Chinese poetic tradition. The finest of the early examples of *shi* poems is the set called the *Nineteen Old Poems*, one of which is included in this selection (p. 26). These rather sombre poems deal with themes such as separation, distance and the ephemeral nature of human life.

During the period of disunity known as the Six Dynasties, which spanned the end of the Han dynasty to the beginning of the Sui in AD 589, an anthology of aristocratic love poems was compiled, called *New*

Songs from the Jade Terrace. These often give frank expression to the love between husband and wife while also depicting seductive courtesans, abandoned ladies and their feminine charms. The title of the anthology is a good illustration of one of the prevailing characteristics of Chinese love poetry – the widespread use of allusion and implication rather than explicit references to sex. In this case, the Jade Terrace of the title refers to the apartments where palace ladies lived, but also possibly to a mirror stand of jade used by ladies at their toilette, or even to a part of the female body, for jade often appears in euphemisms for sexual organs in phrases such as jade stem and jade gate. The title therefore communicates a very subtle eroticism.

Chinese poetry reached a climax in the Tang dynasty (618–907), a golden age during which many of the greatest poets lived, such as Li Bai (Li Po), Du Fu, Bai Juyi (Po Chu-yi) and Wang Wei. Poems by all these men are included here, along with examples by two female poets, one a courtesan called Xue Tao who was renowned for her poetic abilities. The number of poems written during this period shows a dramatic increase: the *Complete Tang Poetry* contains over 48,000 poems, and Du Fu alone wrote about 1,400. It was during this time that the seven-character *shi* poem became popular, as did new poetic forms called *jinti shi* or modern-style poetry, in which the four tones used to distinguish words in speech were controlled so as to avoid repetition of characters pronounced with the same tone. The older type, in which the tones were unregulated, was known as *gu shi* or old-style poetry. Rules regulating the modern-style poetry were introduced in the seventh century and demanded, for example, that all rhyming words should be in the same tone. A short four-line poem called *jueju* or 'broken-off lines' was also introduced and widely used, each line having either five, six or seven characters. The *jueju* in its shortest form could be compared to Japanese haiku. Many of the poems written in the Tang dynasty involved parting couples: often the husband had to go away to fight in the wars being waged by expansionist emperors. Li Bai was an individualist, associated with Daoism and famous for his predilection for writing poetry while drunk and communing with nature. He preferred the freedom of old-style poetry but was particularly accomplished at composing *jueju*. Du Fu, by contrast, was a serious Confucian, concerned with human affairs and enthusiastic about the modern-style poetry and its technical demands.

Fewer poems have been included from the time after the end of the Tang dynasty. There were, of course, accomplished poets in the following Song and succeeding dynasties, as well as new forms of poetry such as the *ci* and the *qu* poems, but other forms of literature also developed, such as drama and the novel, and there were no major poets comparable to the great figures of the Tang. However, there was an explosion in the number of poems written by women during the Ming and Qing dynasties, perhaps due in part to the spread of printing and literacy resulting in the rise of a female readership. From the seventeenth century onwards there was a proliferation of collections and anthologies of poems written by women, many containing love poems. An example is 'Song of Meeting You' by Xu Jingfan (Ho Kyongbyon) (1563–89):

> We met below the pleasure house.
> You tied your horse by the willow at the front door.
> Laughingly I took off my brocade and mink fur.
> We reached for the Xinfeng wine.

Certain stylistic devices feature prominently in Chinese poetry, including allusion, imagery, parallelism and stylized language. Allusions are usually to famous events and people from the past which would be well known to the reader, perhaps inducing nostalgia. Imagery is often extremely effective and evocative, as in a poem by Du Mu (803–52), where the dripping candle is described as crying in sympathy with the separating lovers (p. 70).

> Deeply in love, but tonight
> we seem to be passionless;
> I just feel, before our last cup of wine
> a smile will not come.
> The wax candle has sympathy –
> weeps at our separation:
> Its tears for us keep rolling down
> till day breaks.

An example of parallelism can be seen in this short poem by Tao Yuanming (365–427), in which the transience of beauty in nature is a metaphor for the unpredictability of human experience:

> Bright blossoms seldom last long:
> Life's ups and downs can't be charted.

Chinese poetry is frequently personal and often linked to a particular occasion. Almost anyone with an understanding of the rules might write poetry, which could be composed for entertainment at banquets, outings or parties, or exchanged amongst friends at times of parting. Sometimes composing poetry was turned into a game, with participants drawing lots to decide which rhymes to use. A Chinese poem written for a specific occasion may be given a title which includes the time, place and circumstances of its composition, as if the poet wished to record a particular sentiment exactly as it was experienced at that moment. This contrasts with the common Western view that poetry should capture a universal truth or emotion, transcending its immediate circumstances.

Certain topics, such as the change of seasons and the parting of friends, are particularly popular in Chinese poetry. In Confucian teaching, friendship is regarded as one of the five basic human relationships, so it is not surprising that it plays an important role in poetry. Compared to friendship, romantic love was seen as less worthy, although love poems were sometimes addressed to a wife or husband during a period of enforced separation and travel. There are also poems such as the 'Palace Plaint' of the forgotten concubine, by Bai Juyi (Po Chu-yi) (772–846), which express regret for lost opportunities, the passing of time and the loss of youth:

> Tears have soaked her gauze handkerchief
>   but no dreams come;
> Deep in the night, from the front of the Palace
>   she can hear the beat of music.
> Her rosy cheeks are still fresh
>   but she lost the Emperor's favour –
> She sits there, leaning on the clothes-airer,
>   waiting for daybreak.

The love of country, home, family and children are also worthy Confucian subjects for poetry. A poem (p. 88) addressed to his late wife, Yang Kaihui, by Chairman Mao is written in good Confucian tradition.

Chinese love poems are far more subtle and less spiritually intense than in the Western poetic tradition. Women were not adored in the same way and any reference to sex is couched in terms of the utmost delicacy, often by allusion. The women who feature in conventional love poetry written by men, particularly of the Six Dynasties period

Woman with children playing in a garden, late 18th century, Qing dynasty.
Hanging scroll, ink and colours on silk. Children, particularly boys, were traditionally
regarded in China as a great blessing, and many paintings depict 'the hundred children'.
It was thought that the more sons a man had, the better: King Wen (Zhou dynasty,
c.1050 BC) was reputed to have fathered a hundred sons.

Pair of magpies with flowering plum blossom and peonies, 17th century, late Ming or early Qing dynasty. Colour woodblock print.
A pair of magpies is a traditional Chinese symbol of marital joy, referring to an old Chinese legend of the Herdboy and the Spinning Girl. The peony is a symbol of maidenhood and the plum blossom signifies beauty and sexual pleasure.

(220–589), can be palace ladies, wives of officials, peasant women or 'singing house' girls. Most are described as unhappy because of separation, abandonment or unsatisfied desire. In conventional love poems, the lady often appears listless, watching the moon, birds or flowers, which all remind her of the passing of time. She also weeps because of her sadness, loneliness and the meaninglessness of her life without her lover, or so he supposes. Articles of clothing or furniture are often dwelt on in detail. In some cases, homosexual love between men is treated, in which case the same flowery language is used to describe their dress and appearance as in poems about women, suggesting that the same ideals of beauty were applied to both genders. The ideal beauty at this time would seem to be very young – sometimes the age of a girl is mentioned as in her teens. The hair was elaborately done up and usually held in place by jewelled hairpins of gold, silver or jade. Much jewellery was also worn over very thin, flowing silk garments. However, although this might seem to lead to descriptions of the body underneath, in fact Chinese poets rarely describe the breasts or the bottom (in contrast to Indian love poetry). The waist is sometimes referred to as very slender, as are wrists, and the hands are delicate and white. 'Moth eyebrows' were a sign of beauty, enhanced by mascara. Lipstick, rouge and powder were also used, together with beauty spots, all applied in an elaborate and time-consuming ritual. This floating, diaphanous fashion is well illustrated in the *Admonitions of the Court Instructress*, a famous painting often attributed to the artist Gu Kaizhi, who lived during this period.

If Chinese poems deal with romantic and sexual love and express intense and passionate feelings, this is done indirectly because of social conventions, with much use of symbolism. Instead of making direct reference to virginity, for example, a peach or peony might be described. Mandarin ducks, pairs of magpies or fish signify happily married love, while many-seeded fruit such as melons and pomegranates indicate the hope for many children, and cicadas and peaches the wish for long life. All these poetic clues remain as obvious to Chinese readers as would the mention of a red rose in the Western tradition.

Sex would be alluded to only indirectly, as in this poem by Shen Yue (441–553):

> I think of when she sleeps
> struggling to stay awake when others have retired,
> undoing her sheer gown without waiting to be urged,
> resting on the pillow till caresses find her.
> Fearful that the one by her side is watching,
> she blushes under the candle glow.

By the banks of that marsh, there are sweet flags and lotus
There is a handsome man, I am smitten, what should I do?
Asleep or awake I do nothing, my tears flow like rain.

By the banks of that marsh, there are sweet flags and lotus
And just one handsome man, stately and tall.
Asleep or awake I do nothing, in my heart I am grieved.

By the banks of that marsh, there are sweet flags and lotus
There is a handsome man, very tall and grave.
Asleep or awake I do nothing, tossing and burying my face in the pillow.

From *The Book of Songs*

Detail from 'The Edge of the marsh', section 10 of the *Odes of Chen* by Ma Hezhi (c.1131–62), Southern Song dynasty. Handscroll, ink and colours on silk.

If you tenderly love me,
Gird your loins and wade across the Chen;
But if you do not love me —
There are plenty of other men,
Of madcaps maddest, oh!

If you tenderly love me,
Gird your loins and wade across the Wei;
But if you do not love me —
There are plenty of other knights,
Of madcaps maddest, oh!

From *The Book of Songs*

Detail of Heavenly lady scattering flowers, by Xu Mei, c.1700,
Qing dynasty. Hanging scroll, ink and colours on silk.

Deep rolls the thunder
On the sun-side of the southern hills.
Why is it, why must you always be away,
never managing to get leave?
O my true lord,
Come back to me, come back.

Deep rolls the thunder
On the side of the southern hills.
Why is it, why must you always be away,
Never managing to take rest?
O my true lord,
come back to me, come back.

Deep rolls the thunder
Beneath the southern hills.
Why is it, why must you always be away,
Never managing to be at home and rest.
O my true lord,
Come back to me, come back.

From *The Book of Songs*

南
山
之
陽

白玉簫洞露氣浮黃蕊
茶近紫金鈎美人心事
姑人誇挽芳烟惟不下樓
庚寅孟辱
六如居士唐寅

Detail of Lady waiting for her lover, after Tang Yin (1470–1523),
Ming dynasty. Hanging scroll, ink and colours on silk.

Anxiously chirps the cicada,
Restlessly skips the grasshopper.
Before I saw my lord
My heart was ill at ease.
But now that I have seen him,
Now that I have met him,
My heart is at rest.

I climbed that southern hill
To pluck the fern-shoots.
Before I saw my lord
My heart was sad.
But now that I have seen him,
Now that I have met him,
My heart is still.

I climbed that southern hill
To pluck the bracken shoots.
Before I saw my lord
My heart was sore distressed.
But now that I have seen him,
Now that I have met him,
My heart is at peace.

From *The Book of Songs*

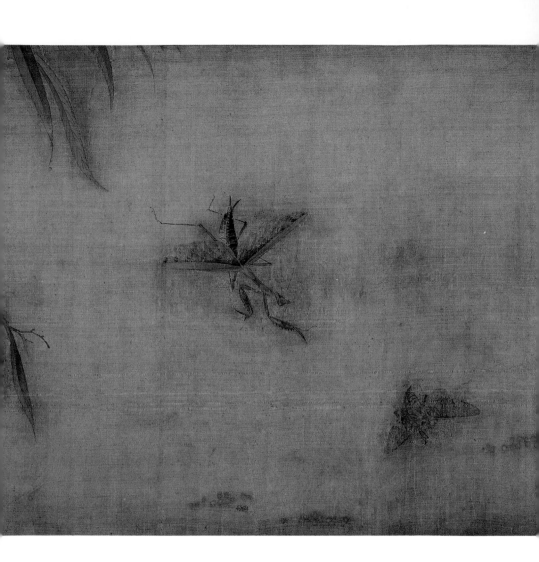

Grasshopper and cicada, detail from Fascination of nature,
by Xie Chufang, 1321, Yuan dynasty. Handscroll, ink and colours on silk.

Do not till too big a field,
Or weeds will ramp it.
Do not love a distant man,
Or heart's pain will chafe you.

Do not till too big a field,
Or weeds will lop it.
Do not love a distant man,
Or heart's pain will fret you.

From *The Book of Songs*

思
遠
人

A Lady looking into the distance, accompanied by her maid,
by Gao Qipei (1672–1734), Qing dynasty. Album leaf, ink on paper.

Sun in the east!
This lovely man
Is in my house,
Is in my home,
His foot is upon my doorstep.

Moon in the east!
This lovely man
Is in my bower,
Is in my bower,
His foot is upon my threshold.

from *The Book of Songs*

在我室

An Official in the doorway of his house,
by Leng Mei (1701–50), Qing dynasty.
Hanging scroll, ink and colours on silk.

Green, green the river-side grass,
Dense, dense the garden willows,
Fair, fair the girl upstairs,
Bright, bright she faces the casement,
Gay, gay her red-powdered face,
Slender, slender the white hand she extends.

Sometime a singing-girl,
Now she is a traveller's wife;
The traveller has departed and returns not,
And a mateless bed is hard to keep alone.

Green, Green the River-side Grass
from *The Nineteen Old Poems*

青
二
河
畔
草

The Broken tryst, by Yin Shi, 19th century, Qing dynasty.
Hanging scroll, ink and colours on silk.

No one can please forever; affection cannot
    be for one alone;
if it be so, it will one day end in disgust.
When love has reached its highest pitch,
    it changes its object;
for whatever has reached its fullness must
    needs decline.
This law is absolute.
The beautiful wife who knew herself to be
    beautiful was soon hated.
If by a mincing air you seek to please,
    wise men will abhor you.
From this cause truly comes the breaking
    of favour's bond.

From *Admonitions of the Court Instructress*
by Zhang Hua (232–300)

歡
不
可
以
瀆

The Emperor rejecting a concubine, detail of Admonitions of the
Court Instructress, after Gu Kaizhi (c.344–c.405), c.5th–6th century.
Handscroll mounted as a panel, ink and colours on silk.

All at once she straightens herself
Skipping this way and that.
To her left a brilliant streamer,
on her right a cassia flag.
O she bares her white wrist at the fairy bank.
She plucks lingzhi from the shallows.
O how my emotions delight in her pure beauty,
Yet my heart is troubled and anxious.
Lacking a good matchmaker to convey my joy,
I consign my words to the gentle waves.
Longing to express my sincerity in advance
I unfasten a jade ornament by way of a sign.

From The Nymph of the Luo River
by Cao Zhi (192–232)

翩
若
驚
鴻

The Emperor catches sight of the nymph and falls instantly in love with her,
detail from The Nymph of the Luo River, after Gu Kaizhi (c.344–c.405),
13th–14th century, Jin or Yuan dynasty. Handscroll, ink and colours on silk.

Flowers bloom:
no one
to enjoy them with.

Flowers fall:
no one
with whom to grieve.

I wonder when love's
longings
stir us most —

when flowers bloom,
or when flowers fall?

Gazing at Spring, I
by Xue Tao (768–c.832)

花
開
花
落

Basket of flowers, 16th–17th century, Ming dynasty.
Album leaf, ink and colours on silk.

I gather herbs
and tie
a lover's knot

to send to one
who understands my songs.

So now I've cut
that springtime sorrow
off.

And now the spring-struck birds
renew their cries

同
心
草

Birds on a flowering branch, 16th century, Ming dynasty.
Hanging scroll, ink and colours on silk.

Windblown flowers
grow older day by day.

And our best season
dwindles in the past.

Without someone
to tie the knot
of love,

no use to tie up
all those love-knot herbs.

Gazing at Spring, II & III
by Xue Tao (768–c.832)

I warn you — cherish not your gold-threaded coat;
I warn you — cherish rather the days of your youth!
When the flower blooms, ready for picking,
     pick it you must:
Don't wait till the flower falls
     and pick a bare twig!

The Coat with the Golden Threads
by Du Qiuniang (Tang dynasty)

Ladies admiring embroidery,
after Chen Hongshou (1599–1652),
late Ming or early Qing dynasty.
Hanging scroll, ink and colours on silk.

Cold is the wind that rises
    over this remote region;
Old friend, tell me your thoughts!
When will a wild goose reach me here
From the rivers-and-lakes
    where the autumn waters are brimming?

Writing is at odds with worldly success,
Forest demons exult to have men come by.
You should join your plaints
    with the spirit of Qu Yuan –
Drop a poem from him into the Mile!

At the World's End, Thinking of Li Po
by Du Fu (712–70)

Gentleman seated alone in a thatched pavilion gazing into the distance,
by Yu Ming (1884–1957) and Chu Deyi (1871–1942), in the style
of Du Qiong (1396–1474). Hanging scroll, ink on paper.

If I want to reach Yellow Flower river
I always follow Green Gully stream;
It coils through the mountains
    with ten thousand turnings,
Hurrying along
    it barely covers a hundred *li*.
What a clamour it makes among the jumbled rocks!
Deep in the pinewoods
    how quiet and still it seems.
Adrift with water-chestnuts, lightly swaying,
Translucently it mirrors reeds and rushes . . .
    My heart is free and at peace,
    As tranquil as this clear stream.
    Let me stay on some great rock
    And trail my fishing-hook for ever!

Green Gully
by Wang Wei (699–759)

Fisherman, by Gao Qipei (1672–1734), Qing dynasty.
Album leaf, ink and colours on paper.

Among the flowers, with a whole pot of wine,
— A solitary drinker with no companions —
I raise my cup to invite the bright moon:
It throws my shadow
　　　and makes us a party of three.

But moon
　　　understands nothing of drinking,
And shadow
　　　only follows me aimlessly.
For the time
　　　shadow and moon are my fellows,
Seizing happiness
　　　while the Spring lasts.
I sing:
　　　the moon sails lingeringly,
I dance:
　　　my shadow twirls and bobs about.
As long as I'm sober, we all frolic together;
When I'm drunk, we scatter and part.
Let us seal for ever
　　　this passionless friendship —
Meet again
　　　by the far-off River of Stars!

举
杯
邀
明
月

Drinking Alone Under the Moon
by Li Bai (Li Po) (701–62)

Detail of *Poet reclining with a cup of wine*,
by Gao Qipei (1672–1734), Qing dynasty.
Album leaf, ink and colours on paper.

A clear moon climbs over the sea;
To its farthest rim
    the whole sky is glowing.
Lovers complain — how endless is the night!
Their longing thoughts rise till the dawn.

I blow out the candle
    to enjoy the clear radiance,
Slip on my clothes
    for I feel the dew grow thick.
Since I cannot gather a handful of moonlight
    to give you,
I shall go back to sleep
    and hope to meet you in a dream!

Looking at the Moon and Longing for a Distant Lover
by Zhang Jiuling (673–740)

天涯共此時

Detail of *Lady resting*, after Zhou Wenju (active c.961–75).
Handscroll, ink and colours on silk.

You came, Sir,
    from my old village –
You must know
    all the village affairs:
Tell me,
    was the winter-plum in flower
Before my gauze window
    on the day you left?

Poem
by Wang Wei (699–759)

Gentleman seated on a rock in a landscape,
under a flowering plum tree, by Weng Pu (1801–50),
Qing dynasty. Hanging scroll, ink and colours on silk.

47

So slender, so supple,
    little more than thirteen,
A nutmeg bud on a twig tip
    when March begins.
On the three miles of Yang-chou road
    with a spring breeze blowing,
And they draw up their bead blinds,
    she is lovelier than all.

春風十里

Given in Farewell
by Du Mu (803–52)

Young girl with a basket, by Tang Qi, c.1814, Qing dynasty.
Album leaf, ink and colours on paper.

A cold rain mingled with the river
      at evening, when I entered Wu;
In the clear dawn I bid you farewell,
      lonely as Chu mountain.
My kinsfolk in Luoyang,
      should they ask about me,
Tell them: 'My heart is a piece of ice
      in a jade cup!'

一片冰心

Farewell to Xin Jian at Hibiscus Pavilion
by Wang Wei (699–759)

Jade cup decorated with plum blossom and dragons,
17th–18th century, Qing dynasty.

There will be moon tonight
      over Fuzhou.
In the women's rooms
      she is gazing at it alone.
From afar,
      I pity my little children:
They do not know yet
      about Ch'ang-an.
In the sweet mists
      her cloud-like hair is damp;
In the clear shining
      her jade-white arms are cold.
When shall we two lean beside
      the filmy curtain
With moonlight on us both
      and the tear-stains dry?

淚
痕
干

Moonlit Night
by Du Fu (712–70)

Seated beauty, by Leng Mei (1677–1742), Qing dynasty.
Hanging scroll, ink and colours on silk.

Tears have soaked her gauze handkerchief
      but no dreams come;
Deep in the night, from the front of the Palace
      she can hear the beat of music.
Her rosy cheeks are still fresh
      but she lost the Emperor's favour –
She sits there, leaning on the clothes-airer,
      waiting for daybreak.

Palace Plaint
by Bai Juyi (Po Chu-yi) (772–846)

Detail of a finely dressed lady, from Bodhisattva,
Guide of Souls, late 9th century, Tang dynasty, from
Dunhuang. Hanging scroll, ink and colours on silk.

Hard it was to see each other —
        harder still to part!
The east wind has no force,
        the hundred flowers wither.
The silkworm dies in spring
        when her thread is spun;
The candle dries its tears
        only when burnt to the end.

Grief at the morning mirror —
        cloud-like hair must change;
Verses hummed at night,
        feeling the chill of moonlight . . .
Yet from here to Paradise
        the way is not so far:
Helpful bluebird,
        bring me news of her!

To . . .
by Li Shangyin (813–58)

Detail of a blue bird with gardenia and lichi, from Gardenia and lichi
with birds, attributed to the Northern Song emperor Huizong (r.1101–25).
Handscroll mounted as a panel, ink and colours on silk.

She is a young woman of matchless beauty
Living unnoticed in a lonely valley.
The daughter of a good family, she says,
But ruined now, with woods and weeds for company.
When battle-havoc raged in the Guan Zhong,
All her brothers met their death there:
What availed their high official rank?
She could not even gather their bodies for burial.
It's the world's way to despise the luckless;
Fortune is like a flickering candle-flame.

Her husband is a fickle, callous fellow
And his new love beautiful as jade.
Even dusk-closing flowers follow their nature;
Mandarin ducks never roost apart.
But he only notices his new love's smile —
How should he hear his old love's weeping?
Spring water runs clear in the hills
But away from the hills it turns muddy.

When her little maid returns from selling her pearls
They pull down creepers to mend the cottage thatch.
She plucks a flower, but not to wear in her hair,
And gathers cypress in armfuls.
Her sky-blue sleeves are thin for the cold air;
In the twilight, she still stands beside the tall bamboos.

The Beauty
by Du Fu (712–70)

Girl holding a flower,
attributed to Zhang Ji,
late 15th century, Ming
dynasty. Hanging scroll,
ink and colours on silk.

59

From the clouds we remember her garments,
      in the flowers see her face;
A spring wind sweeps the balustrade,
      pearls of dew lie thick.
If you find her not on the mountain of Many Jewels,
You will meet her by moonlight
      in the Palace of Jasper.

月
下
逢

Song of Qingping
by Li Bai (Li Po) (701–62)

Seated beauty with dog, amongst flowering shrubs, 19th century,
Qing dynasty. Woodblock print, ink and colours on paper.

On the wu-tung tree, phoenix and mate
        grow old together;
Duck and drake cleave to each other
        till death.
A chaste wife will gladly die with her husband,
Taking leave of life
        like drake and phoenix.
She will not break faith
        like the changeable sea waves:
A wife's heart is like the water
        in an old well.

古井水

The Chaste Wife
by Meng Jiao (751–814)

Family portrait in a garden setting, 18th century,
Qing dynasty. Hanging scroll, ink and colours on silk.

Evening rays
        have passed the western peaks —
In a cluster of valleys
        it is suddenly dark.
Moon over the pines
        brings the cool of night,
Wind and stream fill my ears
        with clear sound.

Returning woodcutters
        are almost gone,
In the mist, birds are just
        settling to roost;
You promised
        to come to me tonight —
I am waiting with a lute
        on the path of vines.

On Staying at my Tutor's Mountain Retreat and
Waiting in Vain for my Friend Ding
by Meng Haoran (689–740)

Detail from Taking a lute to visit a friend,
attributed to Jiang Song (fl.c.1500), Ming dynasty.
Hanging scroll, ink and colour on silk.

Phoenix tails on scented silk,
      filmy fold on fold;
Blue pattern on round canopy
      she stitches deep in the night.
A moon-shaped fan
      could hardly hide her blush,
His coach rumbled by like thunder –
      words could not reach her.

It is still and lonely now,
      the glowing wick burnt black;
No message comes
      though pomegranate flowers are red.
A dappled horse is just tethered
      at the bank of trailing willows –
Where should she wait for a favourable wind
      to blow from the south-west?

To . . .
by Li Shangyin (813–58)

石
榴
紅

Lady with phoenix, attributed to Wu Wei (1459–1509)
or Zhang Lu (c.1490–1563), Ming dynasty.
Hanging scroll, ink and colours on silk.

You came to China, a follower of Pratvaya;
The way you travelled was like a path in a dream.
Afloat on grey seas to the sky's rim,
You are leaving now in a light boat of *dharma*.

Moon and wave partake of the Buddhist peace,
Fish and dragon hear you chanting sutras.
I watch with compassion the spark of your single lamp
Clear shining to my eyes a thousand leagues away.

Farewell to a Buddhist Monk Returning to Japan
by Qian Qi (8th century)

水
月
通
禪
宗

Buddhist monk, 8th–9th century, Tang dynasty.
Fragment of a painting from Dunhuang, ink and colours on silk.

Deeply in love, but tonight
　　we seem to be passionless;
I just feel, before our last cup of wine
　　a smile will not come.
The wax candle has sympathy —
　　weeps at our separation:
Its tears for us keep rolling down
　　till day breaks.

蜡
烛
有
心

Given in Farewell
by Du Mu (803–52)

Lady slumped over a stool, accompanied by her maid
holding a candle, by Zhu Yiding (c.1647–1713), Qing dynasty.
Ink and colours on paper, mounted as a panel.

Outside Yongjin Gate the willows are like smoke,
On the Lady of the West's lake the water pats the sky.
Arms jade-white and damask-skirted couples wave the oar,
Mandarin duck and drake fly near the lotus-pickers' boat.

On a Summer Day Remembering West Lake
by Yu Qian (1398–1457)

柳
如
煙

Bamboo and mandarin ducks beside a lake,
by Wang Sunyi, 17th–18th century, Qing dynasty.
Hanging scroll, ink and colours on silk.
Mandarin ducks are a traditional Chinese
symbol of marital fidelity.

Should wives weep
For absent
Husbands, when jade mirrors bear
Dust, when sewing no longer
Suffices, when bracelets come
Loose, when foreheads are
Wrinkled? I say yes!

Tears from the Boudoir
by Guan Hanqing (c.1220–c.1300)

Lady weeping at parting from her husband, 17th century,
Qing dynasty. Colour woodblock print on paper.

Awake from
Morning dreams,
Make-up still caked, I miss my
Young man. Long absent, he brings
To mind, blue
Rivers, ripe
Fruit, green grass.

Sadness in Spring
by Zhang Keqiu (fl.c.1279–1368)

晓
夢
雲

Young lady plucking a flower, with a friend, by Tang Qi, c.1814,
Qing dynasty. Album leaf, ink on paper.

Despite west winds, come welcomed geese.
One thinks of the sad fates of
Past dynasties. Scribe the clean
Paper with sweet songs of sadness!
Genius fails my quick
Brush. Tired, today, I
Write only
Of mutual love.

Written for Someone
by Guan Yunshi (fl.1312–21)

相
思

Lady seated writing in a pavilion, by Wan Shouqi (1603–52),
late Ming dynasty. Album leaf, ink and colours on silk.

Three slow years have gone by, my tearful eyes
    have dried up,
Although alive I seem dead – how much more
    this hurts me!
Having tasted bitterness deeply, I know the
    hollowness of human affairs,
I envy those sleeping in peace in the world of the dead.
The cuckoo survives, weeping for its millennial pain:
It might change into a crane and return once and for all to the void.
I suppress my grief, supervise the libation and vegetarian offerings,
Then return to teaching the two little orphans at my knees.

The Tenth of the First Month is the Anniversary of
My Husband's Death; I Wrote this after Weeping
by Xu Zihua (1873–1935)

Mother and child, 17th century, Ming dynasty.
Colour woodblock print on paper.

I too have wished not to love
That I might escape love's agony,
But now after much appraisement,
I willingly accept love's agony

A Trifle
by Hu Shi (b.1891), 1919

愛
之
痛
苦

Rock, by Zhu Da (Bada Shanren, 1626–1705), early Qing dynasty.
Hanging scroll, ink on paper. Rocks and mountains were male symbols,
as opposed to the female water. The Chinese word for landscape is *shanshui* or
'mountains and water'. Strangely shaped rocks were collected and admired by
gentlemen scholars, who derived great solace from their contemplation.

If I were a flake of snow
Flitting light and free in the sky,
    I would make sure of my goal —
    I would fly and fly and fly —
On this earth I have my goal.

Not to go to that desolate vale,
Not to go to those dreary foothills,
    Nor to feel sad on deserted streets,
    I would fly and fly and fly.
You see, I have my goal.

In the air I blithely dance,
Making sure that is her secluded place.
    I would wait for her in the garden —
    I would fly and fly and fly —
Ah, she has a clear scent of plum blossom!

Then with body airy and light,
I would gently press close to her robe,
    Pressing close to her soft bosom
    I shall melt and melt and melt.
Melt into the soft waves of her bosom.

A Snowflake's Delight
by Xu Zhimo (1895–1931), 1925

鐵嶺高其佩

Man in the snow with
an umbrella, by Gao Qipei
(1672–1734), Qing dynasty.
Hanging scroll, ink and
colour on paper.

I lost my proud poplar and you your willow.
As poplar and willow they soar straight up
        into the ninth heaven
and ask the prisoner of the moon, Wu Kang,
        what is there.
He offers them wine from the cassia tree.

The lonely lady on the moon, Chang O,
        spreads her vast sleeves
and dances for these good souls in the unending sky.
Down on earth a sudden report of the tiger's defeat.
Tears fly down from a great upturned bowl of rain.

The Gods
by Mao Zedong (1893–1976), on the death
of his first wife Yang Kaihui, 11 May 1957

楊
柳
輕
颺

Girl under a willow with a fish, by Min Zhen (1730–88),
Qing dynasty. Hanging scroll, ink on silk.

Early rays of sun illumine the parade grounds
and these handsome girls heroic in the wind,
      with rifles five feet long.
Daughters of China with a marvellous will,
you prefer hardy uniforms to colourful silk.

Militia Women
by Mao Zedong (1893–1976), February 1961

爱
武
装

Detail of a revolutionary poster, showing the Adoration of
Chairman Mao outside the Forbidden City in the Square of
Heavenly Peace during the Cultural Revolution (1966–76).

bright afternoon
the bugle call over and over
persimmons filling trees shimmer
like knowledge in the mind
I open the door to await night
and in a sage-master's time
read books, play chess
someone on a throne
throws a rock

doesn't hit me
spectral boatmen row past
ripple-light creates you
etches your skin
our fingers intertwine
a star puts on the brakes
shines all over us

柿
子
晃
動

Purple
by Bei Dao (b.1949)

Persimmons, by Fang Zhaoling (b.1914), 1967.
Hanging scroll, ink and colours on paper.

BIOGRAPHICAL NOTES

BAI JUYI (Po Chu-yi, 772–846): A well-loved poet of the Tang dynasty (618–906), he was known for the simplicity of his style, his criticisms of the extravagance of the emperor and his sympathy for the plight of the common people.

BEI DAO (b.1949): Pen name of Zhao Zhenkai. Born in Beijing, he was a Red Guard in the late 1960s and became an underground poet in the 1970s, using unusual and original language, imagery, structure and syntax. He regarded his most famous poem, 'The Answer', as a personal challenge to the political leadership. His work from the 1980s is characterized by bitterness and despair.

DU FU (712–70): A serious figure, generally regarded as China's greatest poet, whose life spanned the highpoint of the Tang dynasty (618–906) and the An Lushan rebellion in 755, after which he fled the capital.

DU MU (803–52): A master of the short *jueju* poem popular in the Tang dynasty (618–906), his work is joyful and sensual.

DU QIUNIANG: A female poet of the Tang dynasty (618–906), her famous 'Ballad of the Coat with the Golden Threads' is also known as 'Congratulating the Bridegroom'.

GUAN HANQING (c.1220–c.1300): He lived in Dadu (Beijing), capital of the Mongol Yuan dynasty (1279–1368), and wrote many operatic plays as well as acting. His poems are mainly about nature or romance.

GUAN YUNSHI: A poet of the Mongol Yuan dynasty (1279–1368) who lived during the reign of the emperor Renzong (1312–21), he became an advisor to the Hanlin (Forest of Brushes) Academy. Originally a Muslim, his grandfather was involved in the Mongol conquest of the previous Song dynasty.

HU SHI (b.1891): Studied in the United States at Cornell and Columbia universities and was professor at Peking University. He formulated his idea of a literary revolution in a periodical called *Xin Qingnian* or *La Jeunesse*. During the war with Japan he was ambassador to the United States, and he left China in 1949 after the Communist revolution.

JI WUQIAN: Lived in the early eighth century during the Tang dynasty (618–906), graduated in the Kaiyuan period (713–42) and was Assistant Minister to the Board of Works. He enjoyed a high reputation as a talented man of letters and a poet.

LI BAI (Li Po, 701–62): Poet of the Tang dynasty (618–906) influenced by Daoism, he was a free spirit compared to his Confucian contemporary Du Fu. He brought new skill and spontaneity to traditional poetic forms.

LI SHANGYIN (813–58): Poet of the later Tang dynasty (618–906) who was known for the ambiguity of meaning and beauty of the imagery in his love poems.

MAO ZEDONG (Mao Tse-tung, 1893–1976): Chairman Mao was well read in the Chinese classics and an accomplished poet and calligrapher as well as a revolutionary and politician. Renowned for his appreciation of female charms, he once said: 'Women hold up half the sky'.

MENG HAORAN (689–740): Failed to pass the official examinations and led the life of a recluse in the mountains during the early Tang dynasty (618–906). Mainly a nature poet, he was friendly with Wang Wei.

MENG JIAO (751–814): A poet-recluse who did not pass the official examinations until the age of fifty, he held only minor civil service posts in the Tang dynasty (618–906). A friend of the great scholar Han Yu, his poetry used rough, direct language.

QIAN QI: Born in Jiangsu province during the Tang dynasty (618–906), he passed the Advanced Scholar examination around 751. He was a member of the Ten Men of Genius of the Dali period (766–80) and was an admirer of Wang Wei.

WANG BO (648–75): A precocious scholar who began writing at the age of six, he was employed by the Tang dynasty emperor Gaozong (r.649–83) to prepare dynastic histories but drowned on his way to Indochina.

WANG WEI (699–759): An accomplished painter, calligrapher and musician of the early Tang dynasty (618–906), his poems are deeply imbued with his Buddhist faith and characterized by a certain passivity.

WEI YINGWU (b.736): A versatile poet-official of the Tang dynasty (618–906), he wrote old-style and modern-style verse as well as *jueju* short poems.

XI PEILAN (1760–1820): A star pupil of the poet Yuan Mei in the mid Qing dynasty (1644–1911), Xi was already admired for her talent and originality when she married at sixteen.

XU ZHIMO (1895–1931): Possibly the best-known Chinese poet of the twentieth century, both for his work and for his 'scandalous' private life which included a divorce and subsequent remarriage to a divorcée. He studied at Columbia and Cambridge universities and became a great admirer of English Romantic literature. On his return to China, he launched the *Poetry Journal* and the *Crescent Monthly* with Wen Yido. He was killed in an airplane crash.

XU ZIHUA (1873–1935): Born into a literary family, Xu was a friend of the revolutionary martyr Qiu Jin and a principal of several girls' schools after the early death of her husband.

XUE TAO (768–c.832): One of the most famous courtesans in Chinese history, she lived during the Tang dynasty (618–906) and learned to write poems when she was eight. She also excelled at calligraphy and often used small pieces of crimson-dyed paper.

YU QIAN (1398–1457): A poet of the early Ming dynasty (1368–1644).

ZHANG JIULING (673–740): A native of Guangdong province, he was an outstanding scholar who in 736 became Chief Minister to the emperor Xuanzong (r.712–56) of the Tang dynasty (618–906). He warned the emperor against the influence of the eunuchs and the rebel An Lushan, but was forced out of office in 737.

ZHANG KEQIU: A poet of the Mongol Yuan dynasty (1279–1368), he was a native of Zhejiang province in southeast China.

FURTHER READING AND SOURCES

Barnstone, Willis (trans., with Ko Ching-Po): *The Poems of Mao Tse-tung*, Bantam Books, New York, 1972

Bei Dao (trans. David Hinton, with Yanbing Chen): *Landscape over Zero*, New Directions, New York, 1995

Birrell, Anne, *New Songs from a Jade Terrace: An Anthology of Early Chinese Love Poetry*, Penguin, Harmondsworth, 1986

Chang, Kang-i Sun and Saussy, Haun (eds): *Women Writers of Traditional China: An Anthology of Poetry and Criticism*, Stanford University Press, 1999

Cheng, François (trans. Donald A. Riggs and Jerome P. Seaton): *Chinese Poetic Writing*, Indiana University Press, Midland Books, 1982

Eberhard, Wolfram: *A Dictionary of Chinese Symbols*, Routledge, London, 1986

Graham, A C. (trans.): *Poems of the West Lake*, Wellsweep, London, 1990

Herdan, Innes (trans.): *Three Hundred Tang Poems*, The Far East Enterprise Co., New York, 1972

Hightower, James R. and Yeh, Florence Chia-ying: *Studies in Chinese Poetry*, Harvard University Press, 1998

Kotewall, Robert and Smith, Norman L. (trans.): *The Penguin Book of Chinese Verse*, Harmondsworth, 1962

Larson, Jeanne (trans.): *Brocade River Poems: Selected Works of the Tang Dynasty Courtesan Xue Tao*, Princeton University Press, 1987

Lin, Julia C.: *Modern Chinese Poetry: An Introduction*, University of Washington Press, Seattle and London, 1972

Liu, James J. Y: *The Art of Chinese Poetry*, University of Chicago Press, 1962

Liu, Wu-chi and Lo, Irving Yucheng (eds): *Sunflower Splendor: Three Thousand Years of Chinese Poetry*, Indiana University Press, 1975

Waley, Arthur (trans.): *The Book of Songs*, Allen and Unwin, London, 1937

Watson, Burton: *Chinese Lyricism from the Second to the Twelfth Century*, Columbia University Press, 1971

Watson, Burton: *The Columbia Book of Chinese Poetry from Early Times to the Thirteenth Century*, Columbia University Press, 1984

Yang, Richard F. S. and Metzger, Charles R. (trans.): *Fifty Songs from the Yüan: Poetry of 13th Century China*, Allen and Unwin, London, 1967

ILLUSTRATION AND TEXT REFERENCES

All photographs © The Trustees of The British Museum, Department of Asia (formerly Oriental Antiquities), courtesy of the Department of Photography and Imaging

page
2 OA 1954.11-13.02, Donated by Mrs REA Hughes-Jones

11 OA 1902.6-17.27, CP 148

12 OA 1906.11-28.09, Collection of Sir Hans Sloane

14–15 OA 1964.4-11.01, Add. 38

17 OA 1910.2-12.0546, CP 181

19 OA 1910.2-12.0511, CP 123, Wegener Collection

21 OA 1998.11-12.01, Purchased with the help of the NACF

23 OA 1951.4-7.02(05), Add. 272, Donated by George de S. Barrow

25 OA 1922.1-19.01

27 OA 1910.2-12.0512

29 OA 1903.4-8.01, CP 1

31 OA 1930.10-15.02, Add. 71, Purchased with the help of the NACF

33 OA 1936.10-9.011, Add. 90

35 OA 1936.10-9.058, Add. 138

37 OA 1936.10-9.019, Add. 98

39 OA 1993.12-25.023, Add. 589, Donated by Robert H. Ellsworth

41 OA 1951.4-7.02(07), Donated by George de S. Barrow

43 OA 1951.4-7.02(03), Donated by George de S. Barrow

45 OA 1963.12-14.02, Add. 336

47 OA 1902.6-6.051,CP 325

49 OA 1902.6-6.057, Add. 357(9)

51 OA 1930.12-17.12, James Hilton Bequest

page
53 OA 1910.2-12.0466, CP 171

55 OA 1919.1-1.047, Donated by Sir Aurel Stein

56–7 OA 1926.4-10.01, Add. 32, Donated by Mrs W. Bateson

59 OA 1881.12-10.014, CP 138, Anderson Collection

61 OA 1954.11-13.04, Donated by Mrs REA Hughes-Jones

63 OA 1881.12-10.074, CP 290, Anderson Collection

65 OA 1947.7-12.04, Add. 228, Harry J. Oppenheim Bequest

67 OA 1913.5-1.010, CP 84

69 OA 1919.1-1.020, Donated by Sir Aurel Stein

71 OA 1925.1-1.01, Add. 28, Donated by George Eumorfopoulos

73 OA 1936.10-9.065, Add.145

75 OA 1956.7-14.07

77 OA 1902.6-6.57, CP 357(06)

79 OA 1946.4-13.1(10), Add. 219

81 OA 1928.3-23.018, Collection of Sir Hans Sloane

83 OA 1958.12-13.01, Add. 295

85 OA 1910.2-12.0541, CP 238, Wegener Collection

87 OA 1910.2-12.0556

89 OA 2002.8-21.018, Given by Gordon Barrass and Kristen Lippincott

91 OA 1979.10-8.01

Translations reprinted by permission of copyright holders where available: *pages* 14–15, 30 (Roderick Whitfield); 26, 82 (© N. L. Smith and R. H. Kotewall, 1962, pp. 5, 73, Penguin Books Ltd); 32–5 (Larsen, Jeanne, *Brocade River Poems*, © 1987 Princeton University Press); 72 (© A. C. Graham, 1990); 84 (Julia C. Lin); 86–8 (Willis Barnstone); 90 (from *Landscape over Zero*, © 1995, 1996 Zhao Zhenkai, trans. © 1995, 1996 David Hinton with Yanbing Chen, New Directions Publishing Corp., Anvil Press Poetry Ltd).